Food for Life

DESERTS

KATE RIGGS

Published by Creative Education
P.O. Box 227, Mankato, Minnesota 56002
Creative Education is an imprint of The Creative Company
www.thecreativecompany.us

Design and production by Liddy Walseth
Art direction by Rita Marshall
Printed in the United States of America

Photographs by Corbis (Michael & Patricia Fodgen), Getty Images (Altrendo
Nature, Tom Bean, Walter Bibikow, James P. Blair, Tim Fitzharris, Tim Flach,
Jeff Foott, Patricio Robles Gil/Sierra Madre, Gavin Hellier, Mattias Klum,
Michael Melford, Mark Moffett, Marc Moritsch, Klaus Nigge, Tom Vezo)

Library of Congress Cataloging-in-Publication Data
Riggs, Kate.
Deserts / by Kate Riggs.
p. cm. — (Food for life)
Summary: A fundamental look at a common food chain in the desert, start-
ing with the hardy mesquite tree, ending with the opportunistic coyote, and
introducing various animals in between.
Includes index.
ISBN 978-1-58341-826-0
1. Desert ecology—Juvenile literature. 2. Food chains (Ecology)—
Juvenile literature.
I. Title. II. Series: Food for life.

QH541.5.D4R54 2010
577.54'16—dc22 2009004779

First Edition
2 4 6 8 9 7 5 3 1

Food for Life

DESERTS

KATE RIGGS

A GREEN BOOK

A food chain shows what living things in an area eat. Plants are the first link on a food chain. Animals that eat plants or other animals make up the rest of the links.

THE TURKEY VULTURE IS
A DESERT SCAVENGER.
IT EATS THE LEFTOVERS
OF DEAD ANIMALS.

A desert is a hot, dry place. **Most deserts have sand or rocky ground.** It does not rain much in the desert. Plants in the desert get the water they need in special ways.

The mesquite (meh-SKEET) tree has long roots. The roots reach far underground to get water. The tree makes seeds that many desert animals like to eat.

Kangaroo rats eat seeds from mesquite trees. A kangaroo rat is not really a rat. But it is a _rodent_. It has a short body and a long tail. It can store lots of seeds in its big cheeks.

Rattlesnakes eat kangaroo rats. The snakes wait for kangaroo rats to leave their _dens_. Then they give them a _poisonous_ bite. A kangaroo rat is not always easy to catch.

GILA (HEE-lah) MONSTERS ARE LIZARDS THAT EAT DESERT TORTOISES. BIG HAWKS EAT GILA MONSTERS.

Rattlesnakes are not easy _prey_ either. A bird called the roadrunner has to act quickly to catch a snake. A roadrunner can move fast. It rushes at a rattlesnake to take it by surprise.

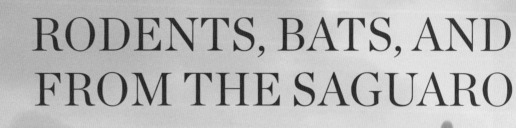

RODENTS, BATS, AND
FROM THE SAGUARO

BIRDS EAT SEEDS
(sah-GWAR-oh) CACTUS.

Wild dogs called coyotes (ky-OH-teez) can smell a roadrunner from far away. Coyotes are faster than road-runners. It does not take long for a coyote to chase down its meal.

THE TARANTULA HAWK IS A WASP THAT LIVES IN THE DESERT. IT EATS SPIDERS CALLED TARANTULAS.

CAMELS DO NOT NEED
THEY EAT SEEDS, LEAVES,

MUCH WATER TO LIVE.
AND SMALL PLANTS.

All of these living things make up a food chain. The mesquite tree grows in the desert. The kangaroo rat eats seeds from the mesquite tree. The rattlesnake eats the kangaroo rat. **The roadrunner eats the rattlesnake.** And the coyote eats the roadrunner.